States of Faith

Poems on Healing

Jen Reich

ISBN: 1460957717
ISBN-13: 978-1460957714

For my mom

Thank you for your faith in me~

CONTENTS

ACKNOWLEDGMENTS

Much gratitude to my teachers and mentors who have believed in me and encouraged me to pursue my writing. Special thanks to Barbara and Larry Dossey, Deva-Marie Beck, Cynthia Sue Larson, Jose Chibras, Patricia Connell, Jackie Levin, Mary Gillepse, Christine Page, Leland Landry, and Linda Held for their support and encouragement of my writing. Thanks to my wonderful friends and the gracious readers of my blog and emails whose support and feedback have kept me writing. I am so grateful~

Author Note

The poems in this book are selections from "poems of the day," that I sent out to my email list between 2008-2011. Usually in these emails I included a little story about my experience along with each poem. I often received responses about the meaningfulness of these stories, and so I have included the original emails next to each poem. Many blessings to all of us on our journeys of healing.

Peace and Gratitude,

Jen Reich

2-24-11

Arizona

In times like this I have to write and pray...I share this
poem and wish you all peace, love and healing~

Tucson, AZ 1-8-11

Prayer for Tucson and the world

When there are no explanations

Please go ahead and weep

The Earth will keep your teardrops

And the sky will hold your prayers-

So when your cares are heavy

And hope seems to be dead

Hold on to the cords of faith

Let the angels kiss your head-

Find comfort in beloveds

Lift each other from despair

For the only way to heal the world

Is to find the strength to care-

I've been struggling a bit with finding my center lately with all the suffering in the heart of the world right now. But even in events that appear distant, I think it is so important to hold a space of peace and healing in our own heart, that this peace may be brought into the world. For me, poetry is a way to pause and sort things out...

Tucson, AZ, 2-3-11

State of the human

Every question doesn't have an answer

Many answers are subjective

But one perspective that I hold as true

Is that you and I are one

So let's lose the guns and words of hate

For they only serve to separate

And if we have to choose a state

May we choose a state of peace~

2-3-11

.

I think this is my second shoe poem, but hopefully this one has a little more sole…

Tucson, AZ 10-10-10

Soles

In your shoes I'll walk a mile

Even if they don't quite fit

And if they're really not my style

I'll simply walk with it-

For your shoes have much to teach me

Your soul upon their soles

And with each stride your beseech me

To understand the whole-

And I'll gladly share my shoes with you

That we may meet a new perspective

Knowing that our worldviews

Are really quite subjective-

And somewhere we will take them off

To feel the Earth between our feet

Grateful that we shared our soles

So that our souls could meet-

10-10-10

Today was chilly and when I got to the pool to swim I was offered an extra towel. Then I had a wonderful conversation with a woman in her 80's who offered me her lap lane in the sun- I carried that energy with me all day- I think sometimes we forget how much little gestures of kindness make a big difference in the world.

Tucson, AZ 11-1-10

The Usual

I headed to bed
Since I needed my sleep
But in the midst of the usual
I started to weep-
I wept for the women
Who spend life in fear
I wept for their babies
Though they could not hear-
I cried for the pain
That persists on this Earth-
And I felt in my soul
That a new day must birth-
So I prayed and I prayed
I begged for a sign
And in the answer that came
I felt the Divine
Calling us to compassion
For all those who live
To know that we always
Have something to give
It might be a smile
It might be a hand
But what comes from one heart
Spreads all over the land
And as long as there's kindness
This world has a chance
But we must lift up our spirits
So that others may dance-

On my walk to the medical library the other day, I found myself reciting the "Hail Mary" prayer of my upbringing. As I entered the building I noticed two display cases I had never noticed, one with painted and poetic tributes to Mary, the other St. Francis and Jude. This poem was inspired by the synchronicity

Tucson, AZ 12-4-10

Full of Grace

Holy Mary,
So many sing your praises
And it's true I go through phases
Where I hear you speak to me-
Though now I see different than a child
No longer tender and mild
My age has changed me
And I've exchanged some views-
But when I see your blues
And angels all around you
I know that I have found you again-
So when I lose my way
I say your prayer
But now it's not for penance
Or in hopes of salvation
For my vocation is to heal-
So I appeal to you to guide me
Walk beside me as I explore
So I can know more paths than one
To One-

This poem woke me up in the middle of the night while I was in AZ, so I felt the need to honor it...

Tucson, AZ 8-14-10

Brave

Will you cry with me?

Not turn away and sigh like there's nothing we can do

Cause I hold the pain of the world and so do you

And we can help each other find our way to peace-

Release the lies that we've been taught

That happiness can be bought and sold-

For the old is dying to make way for the new

To guide us through this shift-

And we can choose to see this as a gift

But either way we all transition-

So let's take the position of love

Rise above perceived limitations

To birth into creation

A world without hate or lack

Where we step back into our power

With the softness of a flower

And the courage of the Divine-

I felt called to send this poem today, as it has been a theme of many conversations with friends and colleagues recently. One of the greatest difficulties in life is to witness the suffering of someone we love, and it is even more difficult when we feel we have a solution or insight into the situation but can't get through. I think many of us have been on both sides of this scenario. The hardest thing for me to remember is that we all must travel our journey...yet we can always be ready to be of service.

Tucson, AZ 2-13-11

Service

It is hard...

When I see your suffering

And I think I can help you

Yet you're not ready to hear-

And maybe it's denial or fear

But who am I to say?

And since we each must find our way

I pray to travel with compassion

For we're all on a journey of healing-

And when we're feeling lost

May we find that help is never far

For we are called upon this Earth

To be of service~

2-13-11

When I was a little kid, I wore thick glasses with a patch on my right eye and would walk with my head down, so no one would see me, and I wouldn't have to look at them. One day, my brother David drew an "eye" on my patch. A kind teacher came up to me and told me how cool it was and how she thought I got my patch off. It was almost 30 years ago, and something I have never forgot. Sometimes I get so self-absorbed into my work that I forget the most important work is to truly acknowledge another being.

Tucson, AZ 2-9-11

Acknowledged

Whether a smile or nod

We find God when we connect

Acknowledge each other with respect

For there is a gift in recognition-

And when we give without conditions

We always receive a greater gift-

A shift in our well-being

Seeing others needs as our own-

For the greatest pain is to feel alone

But it is so easy to rectify

If we never let a day go by

Without touching the divine

That lives within every one

And longs to be acknowledged~

This poem "spoke" to me so I thought I would share...
Take excellent care...

Tucson, AZ 1-11-11

For every heart that seeks

I sense your words before you speak

For in every heart that seeks

There is a common language-

So though our hearts may break

We can make them whole once more-

Open the door and let love enter

Breathing peace into our center-

And when there are no words to say

We'll find our way to healing-

Feeling compassion in our hearts

For every heart that seeks~

California

I was walking on the beach several evenings ago and wondered why no one was there, then I realized it was due to weather warnings- lots of stuff had washed up from buoys to animals. The energy was strange and somewhat sad, and then by the next morning it was completely beautiful, sunny and calm. Anyway, we witness experiences like this all of the time, and I suppose each gives us a chance to evaluate our role in the whole big picture- I do believe we are shifting towards a better place, but try to be mindful that I need to be at peace with now –

Monterey, 10-6-09

Faith

I think the reason that the tide flows high or low

Is to show us that life is always changing

Rearranging itself so we each have a chance

To dance the role of our choosing-

To know there is no losing except for false beliefs

The grief in thinking we are not enough

That stuff is more important than Spirit-

But if we listen close we will hear it call

Like leaves in Fall and birds in Spring

Singing for us to feel and understand

That this land is just a tiny part

Of the heart of our greater being-

And when we start seeing our presence as a gift

The Universe will shift to meet the vibration

Inviting celebration to replace the fighting

Reuniting us with the truth of who we are-

This came to me on a walk the other day- Many Blessings to you all this Easter and Passover week and beyond-

Monterey, CA 3-31-10

Lessons from the Archer

Like the archer I sometimes miss the mark

Yet I know the dark has something to teach me

And it would beseech me to embrace this learning

Rather than yearning for it to disappear-

Still, fear prefers that I stay small

For me to curl into a ball and hide,

But inside me lives a greater being

That is just not into fleeing from fear-

And when I listen to her voice

I make the choice to stand in my power

Shower myself with acceptance and love

Rise above my old limited thinking

And aim for the target again-

I was heading out to the farmers market today when this came to me. I feel a special connection to farmers markets-In the many cities I've moved to knowing no or few people one of the first things I do is go to the farmers market-I've made friends in the baby banana lady in Cleveland, the soap guys in Tucson, and pretzel guys in NYC- Now I am a regular with the goat cheese family in Monterey...

Monterey, CA 12-8-09

Farmers Market

I notice a little baby

And it makes me smile

It's been a while since I've been that small-

I see all the colors of the rainbow

In produce and people walking about

Talking about where to get the best eats-

And though the streets are crowded

There's a sense of community

Unity found in fresh baked bread-

For it might be said that we all are kneaded

In order to rise to our greatest potential-

I took a nice spin in some big surf last weekend and was reminded of an incidence from many years ago. My swim team used to go to Ft. Lauderdale to train each winter and one day several us went out in some strong surf- I got sucked out and was spinning and spinning and this incredible peace just came over me. I swam out of it and let a big wave carry me in- but I will never forget that feeling, and the deep gratitude and respect for the ocean that has been with me ever since....

Corralitos, CA 10-15-10

Current

I got churned and spun

Yearned to be done with the spinning

Yet the water was winning

So I simply released

Made peace with the situation

As I waited to emerge-

And then with a surge I hit the sand

And with feet on dry land

I thanked the water for her gift

The reminder to shift my view

Begin anew with each breath

For aren't life and death and life again

Always a present...

I have a few more days of my comprehensive exams and I have complexity science on the brain... Being in need for a little extra prayer at the moment....I wrote this piece :)

Corralitos, CA 9-26-10

A Simple Complex Prayer

When we are stuck

Please set us free flowing

Into infinite possibilities

Of learning and knowing-

And when we feel alone

Please show us connection

Gifted from wisdom

Of all four directions-

Help us raise our vibration

When we're feeling stressed

In thanksgiving and joy

For a life that is blessed-

Flapping our wings

That each of us soar

Into a space of abundance

Where less equals more-

Certain

In the certainty of uncertain

I pull back the curtain on my fear

Only to hear applause from the audience-

They know a good drama when they see it

Be it from my fear or their own-

And while the unknown can be scary

I've grown wary of its play-

So I pray that I may fully live

Giving from a heart that's clear

That love's more powerful than fear

And I am certain this is true-

10-9-10

32

For every hurt

I don't have a rhyme

for every hurt that ails me

Sometimes pain nails me too-

But what I know is true

Is that we all go through trials

Revisit files in our mind

That we'd like to rewind and erase-

But in any case we have a choice

To use our voices to heal

Feel what it's like to say "I love you"

As we look in the mirror and smile

Walk a mile in the soles of peace

And cease to fire upon our souls-

7-19-2010

I've been wallowing just a tad lately.....so I know I write a lot of poems about the heart- but I am constant need of reminder...

Corralitos, CA 9-18-10

Sum of my Heart

When news overwhelms
And statistics seem bleak
I question my heart
And ask her to speak-
It often takes awhile
To quiet my mind
But when my heart finally speaks
It's just truth that I find-
Because my heart doesn't settle
Her passion is clear
She follows her rhythm
In spite of my fear-
She knows that what matters
Can't be bought with a card
That life can be easy
When I don't make it so hard-
She puts up with my missteps
By keeping the beat
And calls to me gently
To get back on my feet-

I was thinking about the power of words today and this

came to me. Have a beautiful day!

Corralitos, CA 6-14-10

Sticks and Stones

Sticks and stones...

May not always break bones

But callous words can surely maim-

And the names we voice

Reflect our choice

To create peace or hate and fear-

So let's be clear in what we think and say

To collectively create a better way

And shift the paradigm towards love-

That we may rise above the oil

Plant seeds of hope throughout the soil

Knowing that only we can save the Earth-

May we walk in beauty together~

Corralitos, CA 8-20-10

Soul Forest

The forest brings me to my knees

Staring at the trees in awe-

And in this space of raw beauty

I feel the forest within me-

All the bees and flowers

Rain showers on a cool day

Directing a play within my soul

My role no less or more

Than all who've come before and after-

So let me walk in laughter

Swim in song

Knowing that I do belong

To the beauty of it all-

I wrote this today after a conversation last night with my partner Jose about our experiences when we were growing up.... then synchronistically my friend Cynthia sent a beautiful Rumi poem this morning....

Monterey, 11-13-09

Shoes

I've never walked a mile in your shoes

Though my shoes are also worn-

Torn from years of running

From the truth of who we are-

Yet, so far from home we finally pause

To question the laws that we've created-

Realize that we've waited far too long

To hear the song of the Divine

Who is mine and yours the same-

So regardless of the name we choose

We can always let go of our shoes

And return together as love-

Equation

If I am my IQ
The there is no U
For I become a score-
And furthermore
If I am my career
Then it is clear
That my work is number one-
So when the day is done
And I wonder what it's all about
I doubt I'd have much to say-
For the "I" way is a lonely path
And if I must do the math
I'd rather not have to divide
Because inside I know
That I am you, as you are me
And we can be
Uniquely one
Together-

1-30-10

Right Here

If we are love, why do we seek it?

Speak of it as it something we must find

Sending our minds off on a race

To chase after love as if it were:

Food or drink, or clothes or cars

Looking in bars or churches or gyms

And even if we find the right him or her

We prefer to look into future or past

Worrying that love can't last forever-

But though our minds are clever

They are no match for our hearts

That know we are much more than parts

And never apart from the source of love

That is stirring sweetly

Right here-

3-27-10

Illinois

Sort of an odd weekend here in Chicago- rainy, cold after a couple of beautiful days- Anyway, I was doing a bit of journeying and forgiveness work- so this poem is a little different- but I like to mix it up :)

Chicago, 3-7-09

Journeying

I'm so sorry for what's caused you pain

I've got my stories too

I'm so sorry for the pain we've caused

We did the best we knew to do-

Walk with me and shed your tears

The Earth will use the rain

I'll walk with you and shed my tears

Releasing all our pain-

I'd packed a backpack full of fear

And carried it too long

I thought that I was all alone

I know now I was wrong-

For you've been with me on this journey

And we could have shared our pack

Instead of feeling heavier

Our fears holding us back-

So now that we are in the know

Can we let go of some stuff?

The Earth will take it off our hands

She knows we've had enough-

Let's build a fire for our fears

And watch them burn away

Knowing as the flame subsides

So starts a brand new day-

I am sitting at Starbucks wanting a big au lait with mocha syrup (extra hot) but knowing I need sleep :) So I wrote this over a ginger green tea- thinking about the true sweetness of life- Have a lovely weekend- thank you my friends for your sweetness-

Chicago 3-12-09

Sweetness

I am craving sweet-

Not the kind that comes in a bar

Or a good looking car or dress-

While these things impress for awhile

Their style quickly fades

And what I paid is not worth the cost-

But when the frost of illusion clears

My confusion and fears once concealed

Are revealed for me to hear and see

That what I crave is calling me

Showing me a heart divine

With sacred wine flowing through

Connecting you and I as one-

So let the sun shine brightly

And the rain fall down

There's sweetness to be found in all

If we simply call it to us

Allow it to pour through us

And drink-

Yesterday morning at Unity, I heard the story of White Buffalo Calf Woman. It has been told to me on different occasions recently and after hearing it again this morning, I was inspired to write a poem/rap around this great story for the holidays. I know everyone is very busy right now, but as we move into the Solstice, Chanukah, and Christmas season I wish all of you moments of peace and many blessings. Every one of you has made a positive impact on my life and I am grateful. All best wishes to you and your loved ones during this sacred season

Chicago, 12-8-2008

Chununpa

My self
If I allow
To be-
I see
No difference
In another
Sister
Brother
Gay or straight
I feel the shift
And I can't wait
Until
White Buffalo Calf Woman
Comes back to Earth
Healing hearts
With each new birth
We hear the call
To rise above
Reawakening
To divine love
Letting hatred cease
And in its place
Return to peace
And joy
Pure as the baby calf
Like the Dalai Lama
We can laugh
Amidst the chaos
Making way
For the beginning
Of a brand new day
Of life no more
Amongst the storm
With a single note
We can transform
And be free

The babies rest at the very back of St. Boniface cemetery. I noticed this on one of my morning walks through there. There are hundreds of huge monuments from three centuries now, but the tiny markers in the back lay flatly on the earth under the shade of giant trees. I run or walk through the cemetery on most days- to avoid traffic, find quiet, and to feel the presence of the Angels that frequent there, not for the dead, but for the living who grieve them. I had planned on running today, but my heart said walk, and so I took it as wise council. I have learned many times over to listen to this voice. I rounded the corner by my favorite marker- a statue of Mary with her hand on her heart. I wrote a poem about her last week. She moves me deeply.

Chicago, 10-25-08

Mary

Around the second corner
She stands beside the tree,
Her one hand pressed against her heart
While the other arm hangs free
Her head nods toward the grassy earth
But sometimes she looks at me,
I bow each time I pass her
Atop the grave of Cecile Marie.
Sometimes I ask her questions
Say a prayer, or just look on,
I glance and see she's lost a hand
And wonder where its' gone.
Often the geese collect near her
But they never make a sound,
She has a quiet grace to her
That is peace to be around
But I know that she is guiding me
To stay here on this Earth,
She says don't hang around too long
You chose this life to birth
I thank her for her guidance
And I give a final nod,
Though she is just a statue
Through her grace, I talk to God.

Happy Passover and Easter to all!   Yesterday the internet and phone service was cut off in the entire county and it was interesting to notice how reliant we are on technology- I did use the time to write and spent time outdoors.   I am sending this little poem I wrote a couple months ago, as it seems appropriate for the season.

Chicago, 4-10-09

Friendship

I stop and see
My favorite tree
Each time that I head out,
She tells me different stories
Of their truth I have no doubt-

I touch her limbs and feel a surge
Connect me to the Earth,
My tree she doesn't judge me
Or calculate my worth-

In the fall she feeds me apples
In the winter she is bare,
She knows she will bear life again
And new fruit again to share-

I marvel at her calmness
In the midst of wind and snow,
I ask her for her secret
And she simply sways "let go"

I feel my neck and shoulders
Tense and tightened in a knot,
I watch her moving freely
And I realize I am not-

I shake out my whole body
And dance around my tree,
I forget that I am outside
Where anyone can see-

And most would call me crazy
For chatting with a tree,
But I know without her guidance
I would lose my sanity-

So with gratitude I greet her
Each and every day,
I connect with her great presence
Even when I'm far away-

And when I'm feeling in a space
Where no clarity is found,
I imagine I am holding her
With my feet firm on the ground.

These lines came to me on a beautiful walk yesterday-

Chicago 2-10-09

Sacred Heart

Aren't all hearts sacred?

Beating inside

Longing to confide in another

And feel the love of the Mother

That never subsides-

The idea for this little poem arose from a response to *Sacred Heart* from someone I greatly admire-

Chicago: 2-11-09

Jewel

I love Jewelry

Necklaces and earrings

Created of all sorts of things

Some of more value than the other-

But one thing that I've discovered

Lost jewelry may not be recovered

And I can't become attached-

So though the jewels I wear external

Are not eternal

The jewel inside me never leaves-

And when I forget which jewel is more important

It is the jewel inside that grieves.

Ohio

I woke up the other morning with some negative thoughts running through my mind. In these moments, I have learned to pause, take a deep breath, and remember that I am and we are love...

Warren, Ohio 1-2-11

Mirror Speak

I look into the mirror to see

Whose reflection I appear to be-

I first notice flaws and extra hair

Which seems to grow the more I stare-

But in the midst of my critique

Another voice begins to speak

I cannot see her in the mirror

Yet her message comes through soft and clear-

She calls me to look past my shell

To find the space where all is well-

To know that I am born of love

And above all else *to love*-

So though my heart at times will break

There's always healing in its wake-

But I must leave my mirror to see

That you and I are really *we*-

Calling

I was just calling you

As you were calling me

Did we see before we dialed?

In the wilds of space

We found a place to meet

Greet each other in another dimension

Beyond comprehension in standard time-

And isn't it sublime to know

That although we are apart

We are a part of the greater whole

Connected from the soul of the Universe

And called to dance in the vibration

With each other-

6-21-10

Spark

Today I felt a tiny spark

Lighting up my places dark

I saw my fear, my pain, and greed

All waiting for new fuel to feed-

Yet this spark created quite a surge

Enough for new thoughts to emerge

And I knew right then I had a chance

To let go of my circumstance-

To listen to my angels near

To drop the judgment, shame, and fear-

No need to battle, duel or fight

For inside of me lives dark and light

And if within I call for peace

I cease control and join the flow

Knowing what I do not know

Will sometime be revealed~

1-1-11

Walk of Life

There was a time I just forgot

Sought happiness within distraction

And so instead of taking action

I simply fell asleep-

But deep within my spirit stirred

And voices lost again were heard

Angels singing in my ears

Bringing respite from my fears-

For in the story of the birth

We find our time of peace on Earth

Opening to the gifts we share

In every present that we're aware

So as the world cries out in need

With many hungry hearts to feed

May we all find room within our in

To begin the healing journey-

For miracles are waiting

In every walk of life-

12-21-10

Snow Angel Prayer

Snow angel

Though you cannot stay

I pray before you melt away

You remind us of our angels near

To comfort us in times of fear-

And when life seems too dark and cold

Please guide us to the light we hold-

12-23-10

ABOUT THE AUTHOR

Jennifer Reich MA, MS, RN ANP-BC is a nurse, storyteller and poet currently completing her PhD at The University of Arizona. Her background includes degrees in Nursing, Exercise Science, and English/Theatre (minor). Her passion is exploring healing through poetry & story. She blogs at http://www.poetry-not-poverty.blogspot.com/

Made in the USA
Charleston, SC
29 August 2012